YEAR 3

Myths and Legends

KARINA LAW

Teachers' Resource for Guided Reading

A & C Black • London

Contents

Introduction   3

How to Use This Book   4

Target Statements for Reading   5

Pandora's Box by Rose Impey

   Lesson Plans and Activity Sheets   7

Sephy's Story by Julia Green

   Lesson Plans and Activity Sheets   19

Wings of Icarus by Jenny Oldfield

   Lesson Plans and Activity Sheets   31

Record Card   42

White Wolves Interviews   43

White Wolves Series Consultant: Sue Ellis, Centre for Literacy in Primary Education

First published 2007 by
A & C Black Publishers Ltd
38 Soho Square, London, W1D 3HB
www.acblack.com

Text copyright © 2007 Karina Law
Illustrations copyright © 2007 Peter Bailey, Teresa Murfin and Bee Willey

The right of Karina Law to be identified as author and the rights of Peter Bailey, Teresa Murfin and Bee Willey to be identified as the illustrators of this work have been asserted by them in accordance with the Copyrights, Designs and Patents Act 1988.

ISBN 978-0-7136-8520-6

A CIP catalogue for this book is available from the British Library.

This book is produced using paper that is made from wood grown in managed, sustainable forests. It is natural, renewable and recyclable. The logging and manufacturing processes conform to the environmental regulations of the country of origin.

Printed in Great Britain by Martins the Printers, Berwick upon Tweed.

Introduction

What is Guided Reading?

Guided Reading is a valuable part of literacy work within the classroom, bridging the gap between shared and independent reading. A teacher usually works with a small group of children, who are of similar reading abilities, using a text that has been carefully selected to match the reading ability of the group.

The group setting naturally leads to discussion about the book. The teacher's role is to support pupils in their reading and discussion, and encourage them to respond to the text in a variety of different ways, including personal response. In Guided Reading children can put into practice the reading strategies that have been taught during Shared Reading sessions, and the teacher can monitor their progress more closely.

Aims of Guided Reading

With careful organisation and selection of appropriate texts, Guided Reading can:
- improve reading fluency;
- inspire confidence and promote enjoyment of reading;
- deepen understanding of texts;
- provide an opportunity for purposeful discussion, both teacher-led and spontaneous;
- provide a context for focused talk and listening, including role-play and drama activities;
- offer a stimulus for independent writing;
- provide an opportunity for the teacher to monitor the progress of individual children.

The main aim of Guided Reading sessions is to help children become independent readers.

Assessment

Guided Reading is an excellent opportunity to observe and assess the reading strategies used by individual children. When listening to individual children reading aloud, check for accuracy, fluency and understanding, and note the strategies they use to make sense of less familiar words.

The photocopiable record card on p. 42 may be used to record your observations about individual pupils within each group, noting particular strengths and needs. These observations may be used to help note progression and inform your assessment of children's reading development.

Ongoing assessment will also help you to identify when Guided Reading groups need to be reorganised. Children progress at different rates; those who are progressing more rapidly may benefit from reading more challenging texts, while children who are struggling may need opportunites to read more supportive texts.

How to organise Guided Reading

Many teachers find it helpful to organise daily, dedicated Guided Reading sessions to ensure an uninterrupted focus on the group. It works well if each session has a teaching sequence, and the suggestions in this guide offer a structure that you can draw on to make the most of each text and the learning opportunities within them.

Ideally, each group should have a session of Guided Reading every week. Other children in the class can be engaged in a variety of purposeful, independent activities, such as working on an activity relating to a previous Guided Reading session, carrying out reading journals, or paired reading with books of their own choice.

How to Use This Book

Teaching sequences

This guide outlines five teaching sequences to support the use of three Year 3 books with a Guided Reading group:

Pandora's Box – for children who are inexperienced readers

Sephy's Story – for children who have an average level of reading ability

Wings of Icarus – for more experienced readers.

The teaching sequences take into account important elements of reading at Year 3. However, they will need to be adapted to take into consideration the specific needs of individual children within a group to ensure engagement and progress.

The teaching sequences have been planned to be approximately 30 minutes in length, although this will vary depending on how many of the ideas for "Returning to the text" you choose to include.

Independent reading

Each Guided Reading session is likely to be a combination of silent reading, reading aloud and discussion about the text, with the emphasis on reading for meaning. It will be important to hear all children read aloud at some point during the session in order to monitor their progress. However, less-experienced readers will probably need to spend more time reading aloud each session as they are likely to require a higher level of support developing fluency.

Fluency and understanding are both important in reading. Modelling how to read a sentence, with appropriate phrasing and expression, may help children to make sense of the text. Guided Reading offers many opportunities for word and sentence level work but any significant difficulties demonstrated by individual children should be noted on the record card on p. 42 and addressed afterwards so as not to inhibit the group's understanding and enjoyment of the story.

Returning to the text

The questions and prompts in this section may be used to elicit children's understanding of the text. The questions can be asked either during reading or at the end of the chapter. It is not necessary to ask all the questions, as many of these will be covered in discussion arising spontaneously from reading the text. Encourage children to find the relevant parts of the text to support their answers and ask them to give reasons when offering opinions.

Experienced readers require less "literal" questioning and should be encouraged to develop higher order reading skills, for example prediction, inference and deduction.

Additional ideas for exploring the text further include:

- identifying features such as alliteration, similes, compound words, use of italics and capitalisation;
- opportunities for developing prediction skills;
- a range of role-play and drama activities;
- a stimulus for the activity sheet that follows.

It is important that groups have the experience of a reflective conversation about the book and not a "twenty questions" approach to test comprehension.

Next steps

The activity sheets may be used for independent work either in school or as homework. They offer a variety of ways for children to demonstrate their understanding of the stories along with valuable opportunities for writing for different purposes.

Target Statements for Reading

The NLS target statements for reading at Year 3 will help inform your planning for progression in reading.

Word recognition and phonic knowledge:

- recognise a range of prefixes and suffixes to construct the meanings of words in context.
- recognise the function of the apostrophe for omission and pronounce contracted forms correctly.
- recognise the full range of consonant digraphs, e.g. kn, wr, ph.

Grammatical awareness:

- read aloud with intonation and expression taking account of punctuation, e.g. commas to mark pauses and grammatical boundaries.
- understand how pronouns in first, second and third person forms are used in sentences and apply this information to maintain understanding when reading.
- understand how dialogue is punctuated and laid out, and read with appropriate expression.

Use of context:

- know how language is used to create effects, e.g. adjectives and adverbs for description, and used to create detailed mental images.

Interpretations and response: literary text:

- when reading aloud show awareness and understanding of the different voices in stories.
- discuss the actions of the main characters and justify views using evidence from the text.

Attitude:

- sustain silent reading to include longer, more complex texts.
- draw on knowledge of authors and types of books they write to inform choices.
- read aloud confidently to an audience, e.g. favourite passage from a selected text.

Pandora's Box by *Rose Impey*

About the book

Zeus calls upon two other gods to help him create the first living creatures. Epimetheus makes animals, birds and insects while his brother, Prometheus, makes humans. Zeus is angry when he sees that Prometheus has made Man look like the gods. He did not want Man to think himself equal to the gods; he wants him to worship and depend on them. Zeus forbids Prometheus to give Man any more powers but Prometheus ignores him. As punishment, Zeus chains him to a mountain top where he will be pecked by eagles for eternity.

Zeus plans to teach Man a lesson. He creates Woman, who is clever, beautiful and graceful with many talents. He calls her Pandora. Epimetheus falls in love with Pandora and marries her. Zeus presents them with a wedding gift: a large wooden box with a label saying "DO NOT OPEN". Remembering his brother's punishment for disobeying the gods, Epimetheus hides the box. Pandora, however, cannot take her mind off the wooden box because, in addition to her other talents, Zeus had ordered the gods to give her one weakness: curiosity.

Eventually, Pandora opens the box and in doing so, she unwittingly releases illness, fear, greed, jealousy, cruelty, war and even death into the world. But as Pandora tries to close the lid of the box, she notices a pale, fragile thing in the corner. It is Hope. Pandora lets the scrap of Hope fly out of the box bringing a ray of sunshine into the darkness. Still chained to his rock, Prometheus sees Hope fly past and he believes, for the first time, that one day Zeus might set him free.

"Stop! Stop!" she begged. "I'm sorry. I didn't mean to do it!" But the things went on hissing and buzzing until the noise almost deafened her.

Just when Pandora thought she could not bear it any more, the things stopped buzzing and poured smoke-like through the open window.

Soon they were all gone, out into the world, spreading their horrible powers into every corner.

36

37

Pandora's Box: Teaching Sequence 1

Summary of Chapter One

Zeus calls upon two other gods to help him create creatures to make Earth a more beautiful place. Brothers Epimetheus and Prometheus create forms out of mud and breathe life into their creations. Zeus, however, is very angry when he sees that Prometheus has made Man look like the gods. He does not want Man to think himself equal to the gods and forbids Prometheus to give Man any more powers. Prometheus ignores him and steals fire from the gods so that Man can warm himself and cook food. Zeus punishes Prometheus by chaining him to a mountain top. He then plans to teach Man a lesson.

Teaching Sequence

Introduction

- Talk about the book cover and read the blurb.
- Point out that this story is a Greek myth and talk about any other myths the children are familiar with. What do they know about Greek gods, for example, Zeus?
- Look at the illustration of Pandora's box on the front cover. Ask the children to speculate about what might be inside it.

Independent reading

Ask the group to read aloud Chapter One, focusing on reading for meaning.

- It may be necessary for an adult to read the first chapter to support the children in becoming familiar with some of the challenging names and concepts.
- Help with the pronunciation of unfamiliar character and place names such as ancient Greece, Zeus, Mount Olympus (p. 7); Epimetheus (p. 8); Prometheus (p. 9).
- Discuss less familiar words and phrases, such as *worship, depend, equal* (p. 9), *in the dead of night* (p. 11), *beyond anger, harsh, revenge* (p. 12).

Returning to the text

Develop children's understanding of the story by asking some of these questions either during reading or at the end of the chapter. Encourage them to find the relevant part in the text to support their answers.

1) What is the relationship between Epimetheus and Prometheus? (They are brothers (p. 9).)
2) Why was Zeus angry with Prometheus? (He made Man look like the gods. Zeus did not want Man to think he was their equal; he wanted him to worship the gods (p. 9).)
3) Why did Prometheus ignore Zeus' warning not to give Man any more powers? (He didn't want to see Man shivering in the cold (p. 11).)
4) What adjectives does the author use to describe Zeus? ("Top" (p. 7), "angry" (p. 9), "fierce", "harsh" (p. 12).)

Talk about the concept of a "creation story" as a means for explaining how the world came to be. Do the children think it possible that we started out as clay figures before we were given life?

Think about the gift of fire that Prometheus gave to Man to keep him warm and enable him to cook food. In what other ways is fire useful to man? For example, it provides light, it can be used for defence against wild animals, and it can be used to boil water for drinking and cleaning.

Talk about the character of Prometheus. Why does he disobey Zeus and what does this tell us about him? Discuss the severity of the punishment that Zeus inflicts. What does this tell us about "Top God" Zeus? What do the children think he means when he says "Man will suffer for this" (p. 12)?

Next steps

The children can now complete Activity Sheet 1: "The Gift of Fire", which asks them to consider the benefits of Prometheus's gift to Man.

The Gift of Fire

Prometheus loved Man so much that he gave him the gift of fire. Write down all the different ways that fire is useful to Man.

Man can use fire to:

■ keep warm

■ _____

■ _____

■ _____

■ _____

■ _____

■ _____

If you were a god, what gift would you have given to Man and why?

_____

_____

_____

_____

_____

_____

_____

Pandora's Box: Teaching Sequence 2

Summary of Chapter Two

As part of his plan to teach Man a lesson, Zeus creates Woman. Pandora, as she is called, has many talents. As soon as Epimetheus sees her, he falls in love and they marry. All the gods send wedding presents. Zeus sends a box labelled: "DO NOT OPEN". Pandora wants to open the box, but Epimetheus remembers his brother's punishment and hides it in a corner of the house. Pandora cannot take her mind off it; as well as her talents, she has been given one weakness: curiosity.

Teaching Sequence

Introduction

Recap on what Prometheus did to anger Zeus.

Zeus plans to "teach Man a lesson he would never forget"; what sort of plan do the children think he has in mind?

Independent reading

Ask the group to read aloud Chapter Two, focusing on reading for meaning.

- Discuss less familiar words and phrases, such as *graceful* (p. 16), *suspect* (p. 17), *carvings* (p. 18), *disobey* (p. 19), *goddess* (p. 20), *curiosity* (p. 21).
- What does the author mean when she says that Zeus was "smiling through his teeth" (p. 17)?

Returning to the text

Develop children's understanding of the story by asking some of these questions either during reading or at the end of the chapter. Encourage them to find the relevant part in the text to support their answers.

1) What gifts and talents did the gods give Woman? (They made her clever, beautiful and graceful (p. 16); they gave her the ability to sew, cook, sing and play music (p. 15).)
2) What is the meaning of the name Pandora? (Full of talents (p. 16).)

3) How did Epimetheus react when he met Pandora? (He instantly fell in love with her and married her (p. 17). He had forgotten his brother's warning never to trust Zeus and didn't suspect a thing.)
4) Why was Pandora unable to persuade her husband to open the wooden box? (Epimetheus had not forgotten what had happened to his brother; he did not want to disobey the gods for fear of being punished (p. 19).)
5) Explain the expression "out of sight, out of mind" (p. 20).

Look at the use of upper-case letters and italics. For example, upper-case letters are used to emphasise the importance of the instruction: "DO NOT OPEN" (p. 18); italics are used to emphasise particular words: "The box *may* have been out of sight, but it was *not* out of Pandora's mind" (p. 21). Demonstrate how the italics should be interpreted when reading the sentence aloud.

Think about the ways in which curiosity could be considered a negative characteristic (for example, discuss well-known expressions such as "curiosity killed the cat"; "mind your own business") and ways in which it could be considered a strength (for example, curiosity is an essential quality in a detective or a scientist).

Ask the children to role-play the parts of Epimetheus and Pandora in pairs, with Pandora trying to convince her husband to open the wooden box that has been given to them by Zeus.

Next steps

Using Activity Sheet 2: "Let's Look Inside!" children can write the words spoken by Pandora and Epimetheus that convey the couple's different viewpoints about whether the box should be opened or remain closed.

Let's Look Inside!

Pandora wants to open the wooden box that they received from Zeus. Epimetheus is worried about what will happen if they do! Write down what Pandora and Epimetheus are saying to each other.

Do you think Pandora and Epimetheus should open the box? Why?

_____

_____

_____

_____

White Wolves Teachers' Resource
for Guided Reading Year 3
Myths and Legends
© A & C Black 2007

Pandora's Box: Teaching Sequence 3

Summary of Chapter Three

To begin with, married life for Epimetheus and Pandora seems perfect. Pandora makes Epimetheus very happy. Pandora, however, is not happy; she cannot stop thinking about the box she has been forbidden to open. Finally, she decides to open it and keep her actions secret from Epimetheus. As she removes the cloth, Pandora hears noises coming from the box as if something is trapped inside, trying to get out.

Teaching Sequence

Introduction

Ask the children to summarise what has happened so far in just three sentences. For example: Prometheus angered Zeus by creating Man in his image and was chained to a mountain top as a punishment; Zeus created the first woman, Pandora, and Epimetheus married her; Zeus gave a wooden box to Epimetheus and Pandora which he has forbidden them to open.

Independent reading

Ask the group to read aloud Chapter Three, focusing on reading for meaning.

- Discuss less familiar words and phrases, such as *ignore* (p. 24), *exist* (p. 25), *wisely* (p. 26).
- Check that children understand that the "little voice" inside Pandora's head is a literary device used to reveal the character's thought process.

Returning to the text

Develop children's understanding of the story by asking some of these questions either during reading or at the end of the chapter. Encourage them to find the relevant part in the text to support their answers.

1) In what ways did Pandora make her husband happy? (She cleaned, sewed, made wonderful meals, sang and played music. (pp. 22–23).)

2) Why is Pandora unhappy? (She is frustrated because she wants to know what is inside the box and she has been forbidden to open it.)

3) What does the little voice in Pandora's head tell her? (To open the box; it can't hurt to have one look; she can keep it a secret from Epimetheus. The voice represents Pandora's curious nature.)

4) How does Pandora convince herself that it will be OK to open the forbidden box? (She reminds herself that it is half her wedding present and she will keep her actions secret from her husband (p. 28).)

Look again at the ways in which Pandora is a good wife to her husband. How are the roles of wives and husbands different in ancient Greece from married couples living in modern Britain?

Think about the sentence: "But some people, when they're told they *must not* do something, simply *have to* do it" (p. 25). Ask the children what they think about this. Can they remember a time when they were told not to do something and it made them want to do it all the more?

Talk about the "little voice" in Pandora's head. Reread the lines spoken by the "voice". In pairs, children could role-play a conversation between Pandora and the "little voice". "Pandora" can act out her frustration and inability to forget the box. Meanwhile, the "little voice" can try to persuade Pandora to ignore her husband's instructions.

Ask each child in the group to say whether they would open the box if they were Pandora and explain their reasons.

Next steps

The children can now complete Activity Sheet 3: "What's in the Box?", which asks them to imagine what might be inside Pandora's box.

What's in the Box?

"Pandora could hear noises coming from the box. It sounded as if something – or lots of things – might be trapped inside, trying to get out..."

What do *you* think is inside the box? Write down your ideas and then draw a picture in the space provided.

Pandora's Box: Teaching Sequence 4

Summary of Chapter Four

Pandora's curiosity takes over and, despite a sensible voice in her head telling her to walk away and leave the box alone, she decides to turn the key and lift the lid. Within seconds, hundreds of horrible things swarm out and fly around her head. Pandora attempts to close the lid but is unable to do so. Finally the things stop buzzing and pour smoke-like through an open window.

Teaching Sequence

Introduction
Recap briefly on the events of Chapter Three. Read the title of Chapter Four: "The Damage is Done". What does the title suggest will happen in Chapter Four?

Independent reading
Ask the group to read aloud Chapter Four, focusing on reading for meaning.
- Discuss less familiar words and phrases such as *hive* (p. 33), *sweaty-swarming things; Ugh!* (p. 34), *surrounding* (p. 35), *deafened* (p. 36).
- Talk about the meaning of the metaphorical phrase, "she was bursting to find out" (p. 32).

Returning to the text
Develop children's understanding of the story by asking some of these questions either during reading or at the end of the chapter. Encourage them to find the relevant part in the text to support their answers.
1) What did the sensible voice inside Pandora's head tell her? (It told her to walk away and leave the box alone (p. 31).)
2) Why did Pandora ignore the sensible voice? (Curiosity took over (p. 30); the noises called her back and she could not rest until she had opened the lid (p. 31).)
3) In what ways are the "horrible things" in the box like bees? (They swarm, they buzz, they fly (p. 34); the author describes them swarming out of the box "like bees from a hive" (p. 33).)
4) Find examples of alliteration in the author's description of the horrible things. ("creepy-crawling"; "sweaty-swarming"; "scary-scratching"; "buzzing and biting" (p. 34).)
5) What happened after the things stopped buzzing? (They poured smoke-like through an open window, spreading horrible powers into every corner of the world. (pp. 36–37).)

Look at the list of questions on p. 30 and talk about the way that they build up suspense, culminating with the use of the italic.

Find and discuss the similes in Chapter Four: "It was as if hundreds of tiny insects were hissing in her ear" (p. 32); "hundreds of horrible things swarmed out, like bees from a hive" (p. 33); "the things … poured smoke-like through the open window" (p. 36).

Look at the author's use of ellipses on pp. 32 and 33: "Pandora felt scared and almost stopped…"; "She lifted the lid, only a crack…" Talk about the effect of this on the reader; the author leaves the reader hanging on with anticipation about what will follow.

Next steps
The children can now complete Activity Sheet 4: "Horrible Things", which asks them to write a descriptive paragraph about the horrible things that Pandora released into the world.

Horrible Things

Imagine you are Pandora. Write about what happens when you open the lid. Use the descriptions in Chapter Four to help you.

creepy-crawling

sweaty-swarming

buzzing and biting

scary-scratching

I knew I should not have opened the box. I couldn't help it. I just had to know what was inside. Now I wish I could undo the terrible thing I have done. I only lifted the lid open a crack, just enough to peep inside, but then...

_____

_____

_____

_____

_____

_____

_____

_____

_____

White Wolves Teachers' Resource
for Guided Reading Year 3
Myths and Legends
© A & C Black 2007

Pandora's Box: Teaching Sequence 5

Summary of Chapter Five

Pandora realises she has done something bad but she is not aware of the kind of horrors she has let out of the box: illness, fear, greed, jealousy, cruelty, war and even death. As Pandora tries to close the box, she notices a pale, fragile thing in the corner. It is Hope, and asks to be let out. Pandora does so and Hope follows the others through the open window. Still chained to his rock, Prometheus hears the first sounds of pain and suffering. Then Hope flies past and he believes for the first time that, one day, Zeus might set him free.

Teaching Sequence

Introduction

Briefly discuss with the group how they think the story will end. What does the final chapter heading, "The Last Chance", suggest?

Independent reading

Ask the group to read aloud Chapter Five, focusing on reading for meaning.

- Discuss less familiar words and phrases, such as *jealous*, (p. 39), *fragile* (p. 41), *ray* (p. 42).

Returning to the text

Develop children's understanding of the story by asking some of these questions either during reading or at the end of the chapter. Encourage them to find the relevant part in the text to support their answers.

1) What horrors did Pandora release into the world when she opened the box? (Illness, fear, greed, jealousy, cruelty, war and even death (p. 39).)
2) Why had Zeus filled the box with such horrors? (It was part of his plan to punish Man for the actions of Prometheus.)
3) What was the pale, fragile thing left in the corner of the box? (Hope (p. 41).)
4) What happened when Hope was released into the world? (A thin ray of sunshine broke through the dark cloud and Pandora felt less scared (p. 42).)
5) What did Prometheus think when he saw Hope fly past? (He believed that one day Zeus might set him free and began to think of better things to come (p. 44).)

Look at the different titles given to each of the five chapters; do they provide the reader with a clue as to what is about to happen?

Review the themes of the story, for example:
- creation: in what ways is this creation story similar to or different from other creation stories that the children are familiar with?
- obedience and punishment: Prometheus disobeys Zeus; Pandora disobeys Zeus and Epimetheus; how are they punished for their disobedience?
- justice: are the punishments that Zeus hands out just? Is it fair that Man is punished for Prometheus's act of disobedience?
- curiosity: is it a weakness or a strength?
- hope and despair: how will Hope change the world; what impact will he have?

What messages does the ancient myth hold for 21st-century readers?

Next steps

Activity Sheet 5, "Chapter By Chapter", asks children to sequence illustrations from each of the chapters in the text. They are then asked to consider what they would write if asked to produce an additional chapter about better things to come now Hope has been released into the world.

Chapter By Chapter

Each of these pictures is from a different chapter in the story.
Write down what the event is and number the pictures to show
the order in which they happened.

☐

_____

_____

_____

☐

_____

_____

_____

☐

_____

_____

☐

_____

_____

☐

_____

_____

Imagine you have been asked to write a further chapter
about Hope and better things to come. What will you call your
chapter? Write a summary of the things that will happen.

_____

_____

_____

_____

_____

White Wolves Teachers' Resource
for Guided Reading Year 3
Myths and Legends
© A & C Black 2007

Sephy's Story by *Julia Green*

About the book

Persephone (or Sephy as she is called in this story), daughter of Demeter, the Goddess of the Harvest, is out playing when she hears the thunder of hooves. Horses speed towards her and she is swept away. The horses gallop towards a cliff edge, the ground opens up and they are plunged down into darkness. The last thing Sephy sees is water tumbling over rock. She throws her necklace into the water, hoping that her mother will find it and come looking for her.

Sephy has become prisoner of Pluto, King of the Underworld, who wants her to be his wife and bring some light and happiness into his dark and lonely world. At first Sephy refuses to eat, but eventually Pluto tempts her to try the juicy, red seeds of a pomegranate. As Sephy eats the sixth seed, a winged creature appears before her. Hermes is messenger to Zeus, King of the Gods. He tells Pluto that Zeus has commanded him to let Persephone go. But Hermes is too late; Sephy has eaten and anyone who accepts food given to them in the Underworld must stay there for ever.

Hermes leaves the Underworld to consult Zeus about Sephy's fate, and at last he returns with her mother. Zeus has decided that, as Sephy ate only six pomegranate seeds, she must spend six months of each year in the Underworld with Pluto. For the other six months, however, she can live with her mother and help her to care for the trees, flowers and crops. During the time Sephy spends with Pluto, Demeter is sad and nothing on earth grows. But when the six dark months are over, Sephy can creep back up the dark tunnels of the earth towards the pale light of spring and life can begin again.

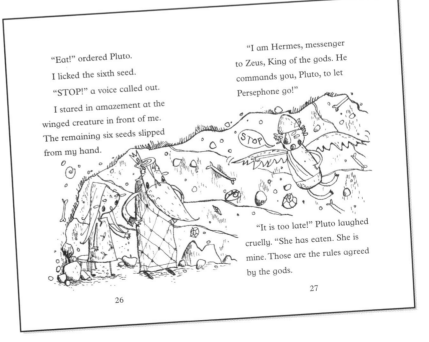

"Eat!" ordered Pluto.

I licked the sixth seed.

"STOP!" a voice called out.

I stared in amazement at the winged creature in front of me. The remaining six seeds slipped from my hand.

26

"I am Hermes, messenger to Zeus, King of the gods. He commands you, Pluto, to let Persephone go!"

"It is too late!" Pluto laughed cruelly. "She has eaten. She is mine. Those are the rules agreed by the gods.

27

Sephy's Story: Teaching Sequence 1

Summary of Chapter One

While Demeter works in the vegetable garden, her daughter Sephy plays in the fields. Suddenly, Sephy hears a strange sound and a cart speeds towards her. Sephy is swept up by a man in black and is unable to escape. They gallop towards a cliff edge, then the ground opens up and they plunge down into darkness. Sephy throws her necklace into the water, hoping her mother will find it.

Teaching Sequence

Introduction
Talk about the book cover and read the blurb.

- Point out that this story is a Greek myth and talk about any other myths the children are familiar with. What do they know about Greek gods, for example, Zeus?

- Look at the illustration on the front cover. Ask the children to talk about the two characters and discuss the contrasts, e.g. light / dark and life / death.

Independent reading
Ask the group to read aloud Chapter One, focusing on reading for meaning.

Help children with the pronunciation of the names Persephone and Demeter.

Find out whether children are familiar with olive groves (p. 8) and pomegranate fruit (p. 6).

Discuss less familiar words such as *harvest* (p. 8), *threaded* (p. 9), *urged*, *orchard* (p. 11), *shrivelled* (p. 12).

Returning to the text
Develop children's understanding of the story by asking some of these questions either during reading or at the end of the chapter. Encourage them to find the relevant part in the text to support their answers.

1) How do Sephy and her mother usually spend their days? (Sephy plays in the fields while her mother works in the vegetable garden (p. 7).)

2) What is a "pomegranate"? (It is a pink fruit full of juicy, red seeds (p. 9).)

3) What is Sephy's first thought as the cart pulled by horses speeds towards her? (She thinks about escaping but decides that it is too far to run to the house, garden or orchard (p. 11).)

4) Does Sephy put up a fight when she is captured? (Yes, she kicks and struggles and tries to escape (p. 11) but the man grips her tightly.)

Note how the mood of the chapter falls into two halves. Look at how the structure of the writing changes in the last three pages. The author uses short lines that contrast with the narrative style of the opening, for example: *I screamed* (p. 11); *Then everything went black* (p. 13). The author's use of repetition helps to build up a sense of suspense, for example: *Closer, closer they came*; (p. 11); *We plunged down, down, down, into darkness* (p. 12).

Discuss how the tone of the writing also changes. It is now creepy and sinister. Ask the children to pick out examples of creepy adjectives and phrases, for example: *dark shadow*; *Ice-cold hands grabbed me* (p. 11). The idyllic picture built up in the first three pages is shattered by this change.

Notice how many of the sentences on the final three pages begin with the pronoun "I", for example: *I was swept up into the cart*; *I kicked and struggled…*; *I screamed* (p. 11). Discuss its effect. For example, it helps the reader understand Sephy's fear; by writing the story in the first person, the reader is able to "see" the things that she saw on her terrifying journey.

Next steps
The children can now complete Activity Sheet 1: "Taken", which asks them to think about the effect of particular words and phrases in an extract from Chapter One.

Taken

Read this extract from *Sephy's Story*. Underline the words and phrases the writer has used to make this part of the story feel creepy and scary.

Suddenly I heard the strangest sound. It was like wind at the start of a terrible storm.

I shivered, even though it was hot. I stood up to see better. A cart, pulled by horses, was speeding over the bumpy ground. It threw a dark shadow over everything it passed. A man in black urged the horses towards me. Closer, closer they came.

Where could I run? It was too far to the garden or our house or the orchard.

Ice-cold hands grabbed me. I was swept up into the cart. I kicked and struggled but the man gripped me tight with one hand. With the other, he whipped the horses faster.

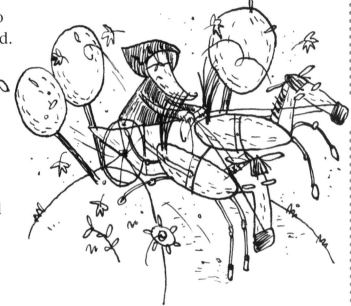

I screamed.

The leaves on the trees turned red and gold as we passed. They shrivelled and curled up as if they were on fire. I watched in horror as the horses galloped towards the cliff edge.

Imagine you are Sephy. Write down how you would have felt when you were carried off in the cart. Would you have acted any differently?

_____

_____

_____

_____

_____

White Wolves Teachers' Resource
for Guided Reading Year 3
Myths and Legends
© A & C Black 2007

Sephy's Story: Teaching Sequence 2

Summary of Chapter Two

Sephy wakes in a huge, underground cave. Footsteps approach. It is Pluto, "King of the Underworld". Pluto tells her that he has brought her to his kingdom to be his wife and make him happy. He explains that his world is dark and lonely whereas Sephy is full of life and can bring light and happiness into his underground kingdom. Sephy questions how she can ever be happy in his cold, dark world away from everyone she loves.

Teaching Sequence

Introduction
Recap on the events of the first chapter. What sort of world has Sephy left behind? What signs in Chapter One suggest that she is going to a very different place?

Independent reading
Ask the group to read aloud Chapter Two, focusing on reading for meaning.
- Discuss less familiar words and phrases such as *stomach, stale* (p. 14), *Underworld* (p. 16), *shrank back* (p. 17), *ledge* (p. 19).
- What do the children know about the Greek god Pluto?

Returning to the text
Develop children's understanding of the story by asking some of these questions either during reading or at the end of the chapter. Encourage them to find the relevant part in the text to support their answers.
1) How does Sephy feel when she wakes at the beginning of Chapter Two? (She is cold, hungry, thirsty and confused; her heart beats faster when she hears footsteps (p. 14).)
2) What simile does the author use to describe the shadows in the flickering light? ("I watched the shadows dance like ghosts" (p. 15).)
3) How does Pluto behave towards Sephy? (He is friendly towards her; he tells her he is happy she is there (p. 16); he tells her he will bring food and drink to celebrate her arrival.)
4) How does Sephy respond to Pluto? (She shrinks back in horror when he takes her hand (p. 17). She is furious with him for stealing her away from her home (p. 18).)

Discuss how atmospheric the writing is at the beginning of Chapter Two. Ask the children to consider the sights, smells, sounds and sensations that the author refers to on the first two pages. What effect does this achieve? Is the Underworld presented as a welcoming place?

Discuss the different sides to Pluto's character? We have seen how he behaved towards Sephy. Is he wrong to want her for himself? Do you think his kindness is genuine? Encourage children to find examples in the text to support their opinions.

How does Sephy's outburst at the top of p. 18 compare with her pleas at the end of the chapter? (Sephy's outburst shows that she is furious and indignant. At the end of the chapter, Sephy's fury is replaced by fear. Her demands turn to a desperate plea: Please let me go.)

Ask the children to look for antonyms in the first two chapters of Sephy's story, for example, light / dark, happy / sad, hot / cold, dry / damp.

Next steps
The children can focus on the contrasts between Sephy's island and Pluto's underground kingdom, using Activity Sheet 2: "Light and Dark". As a follow-up activity, children could identify antonyms and synonyms among the words they have recorded on their activity sheets.

Light and Dark

Find words and phrases in Chapters One and Two that show the contrast between Sephy's sunny island and Pluto's dark, underground kingdom. Include ones that describe Sephy and Pluto themselves.

- ■ full of life

- ■ pretty

- ■

- ■

- ■

- ■

- ■

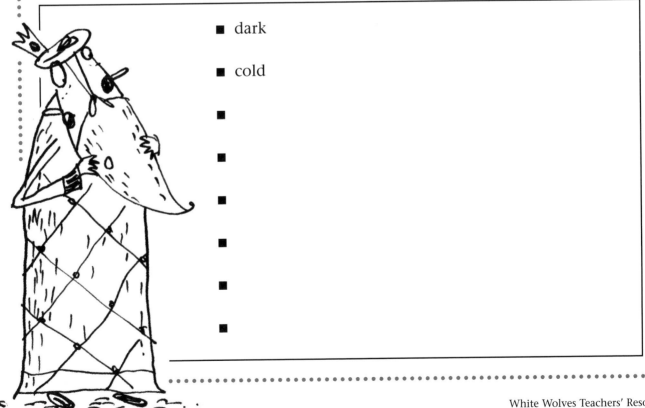

- ■ dark

- ■ cold

- ■

- ■

- ■

- ■

- ■

White Wolves Teachers' Resource
for Guided Reading Year 3
Myths and Legends
© A & C Black 2007

Sephy's Story: Teaching Sequence 3

Summary of Chapter Three

Pluto tells Sephy he will share all his riches with her. Sephy complains that the fossilised treasures are all dead and she can never be happy living underground. Time passes slowly and she refuses to eat, so becoming weak with hunger and thirst. Eventually, Pluto tempts her with a pomegranate. As Sephy tastes the sixth seed, Hermes, messenger to Zeus, appears. He tells Pluto that Zeus has commanded him to let Persephone go. But Hermes is too late; Sephy has eaten and anyone who accepts food in the Underworld must remain there for ever.

Teaching Sequence

Introduction
Ask the children to recap what they learned about Pluto and his underground kingdom in the previous chapter. Why has he taken Sephy prisoner?

Independent reading
Ask the group to read aloud Chapter Three, focusing on reading for meaning.
- Discuss less familiar words and phrases such as *veins in the rock*, *precious* (p. 21), *relics* (p. 22), *almonds*, *figs* (p. 23), *ripe*, *tongue*, *whirring* (p. 25).
- Demonstrate how to pronounce the names of the Greek gods Hermes and Zeus (p. 27).

Returning to the text
Develop children's understanding of the story by asking some of these questions either during reading or at the end of the chapter. Encourage them to find the relevant part in the text to support their answers.
1) Why is Sephy unable to tell whether it is night or day (p. 21)? (It is always dark in Pluto's underground kingdom.)
2) What sort of treasures can be found in the Underworld? (Gold, silver, precious stones, copper, iron and the fossilised remains of creatures and plants (pp. 21–22).)
3) Why did Sephy become weak? (She refused the food that Pluto offered, saying that she would rather die than eat his what he brought for her (p. 23).)
4) What did the pomegranate remind Sephy of? (She remembered the picnic that she and her mother had made on the day she was captured.)

Think about the "treasures" Pluto shows Sephy. Do you think they are valuable or, like Sephy, would you describe them as "ghosts and shadows of living things". Would they make you happy?

Discuss Pluto's behaviour towards Sephy in Chapter Three. Notice especially his behaviour at the end of the chapter when he "laughed cruelly" and declared, "She has eaten. She is mine". Ask the group to consider whether the kindness that Pluto has shown Sephy up to this point has been genuine, or just part of his plan to trap her for ever in his underground kingdom. Encourage the children to find examples in the text to support their opinions.

Children could re-enact the scene that takes place in Chapter Three, where Pluto tempts Sephy to eat the pomegranate seeds, Hermes appears with a message from Zeus and the three characters are left with a dilemma.

Next steps
The children can now complete Activity Sheet 3: "Pluto: Good God or Bad?", which focuses on the character of Pluto.

Pluto: Good God or Bad?

Look at the adjectives below. They describe the character of Pluto at different points in the story. Look back at the first three chapters and find an example in the text to illustrate each adjective. One has been done for you.

cruel   "It is too late!" Pluto laughed cruelly. "She has eaten. She is mine."

friendly   _____

_____

sad   _____

_____

lonely   _____

_____

powerful   _____

_____

What other words and phrases would you use to describe Pluto, King of the Underworld?

_____

_____

_____

_____

White Wolves Teachers' Resource
for Guided Reading Year 3
Myths and Legends
© A & C Black 2007

Sephy's Story: Teaching Sequence 4

Summary of Chapter Four

Sephy is horrified to learn that by eating six pomegranate seeds she is doomed to stay in the Underworld for ever. She hears that Demeter saw her necklace floating on the river and, realising what had happened, went to ask Zeus for help. Zeus sent his messenger, Hermes, to the Underworld to bring Sephy back. Hermes tells Sephy that now she has eaten, he cannot take her with him, but he will try to help. He will return once Zeus has told him what should be done.

Teaching Sequence

Introduction

Recap briefly on the events of Chapter Three. What do the children think of Pluto now that they have learned of his plan to trick Sephy into staying with him in the Underworld for ever?

Independent reading

Ask the group to read aloud Chapter Four, focusing on reading for meaning.

- Discuss less familiar words and phrases such as *shrivelled* (p. 31), *sulked and stormed, fate* (p. 36).

Returning to the text

Develop children's understanding of the story by asking some of these questions either during reading or at the end of the chapter. Encourage them to find the relevant part in the text to support their answers.

1) Why did Zeus send Hermes to find Sephy? (Because Sephy's mother had stopped looking after the crops; the flowers and vegetables had stopped growing and leaves were falling from the trees (p. 31).)

2) How did Sephy's mother find out that Sephy had been trapped underground by Pluto? (She found Sephy's necklace floating on the river (p. 32).)

3) Why can't Hermes take Sephy away with him? (Because the gods agreed that anyone who has accepted food in the Underworld must remain there with Pluto for ever.)

4) How does Sephy feel when Hermes leaves without her? (She is hopeful that she will soon see her mother again (p. 35). She has found new strength (p. 36).)

5) How does Pluto behave while Sephy waits to hear her fate? (He "sulked and stormed"; he is angry that Sephy will eat nothing more (p. 36).)

Look at the author's personification of the river on p. 32: "The river whispered its secret". Discuss how, similarly, the gods themselves represent natural wonders personified. For example, Demeter is the personification of the harvest; when she is suffering, the crops suffer, too. Children could investigate the origins of other Greek gods using books and the Internet.

Talk about the rule that the gods made which stated that anyone who accepted food offered to them in the Underworld must remain there with Pluto for ever. What do the children think about this agreement? Was it fair of Pluto to try to trap Sephy in this way?

Discuss how Pluto and Sephy are now feeling. For example, Sephy feels anxious and unhappy, but is also hopeful that she might soon see her mother again: "even in the darkness, I now had hope" (p. 35). Pluto feels angry that his plan to keep Sephy in the Underworld for ever may fail: "Pluto sulked and stormed" (p. 36).

Next steps

The children can now complete Activity Sheet 4: "Uncertain Times", which asks them to consider how the different characters would be feeling at this point in the story.

Uncertain Times

Think about what the different characters are going through at this point in the story. Write down how they might feel and explain why.

Sephy

I feel _____

_____

because _____

_____

_____

_____

Pluto

I feel _____

_____

because _____

_____

_____

_____

Demeter

I feel _____

_____

because _____

_____

_____

_____

Zeus

I feel _____

_____

because _____

_____

_____

_____

White Wolves Teachers' Resource
for Guided Reading Year 3
Myths and Legends
© A & C Black 2007

Sephy's Story: Teaching Sequence 5

Summary of Chapter Five

Hermes returns and tells Sephy and Pluto what Zeus has decided; as Sephy ate six pomegranate seeds, she must spend six months of each year in the Underworld with Pluto but, for the other six, she can live with her mother and help her to care for the trees and flowers and crops. During the months that Sephy spends with Pluto in his underground kingdom, Demeter is sad and the earth grieves with her; nothing grows. When Sephy creeps back up the tunnels towards the light, life begins again.

Teaching Sequence

Introduction
Briefly discuss with the group how they think the story will end. What will Zeus decide about Sephy's fate? Will she see her mother again?

Independent reading
Ask the group to read aloud Chapter Five, focusing on reading for meaning.
- Discuss less familiar words and phrases, such as *grieves* (p. 41), *limestone* (p. 43), *veins, flutters, peaty soil* (p. 44).

Returning to the text
Develop children's understanding of the story by asking some of these questions either during reading or at the end of the chapter. Encourage them to find the relevant part in the text to support their answers.
1) What decision did Zeus make about whether Sephy should stay in the Underworld? (Zeus decided that because Sephy ate six pomegranate seeds, she should spend six months of each year with Pluto and the other six months with her mother (p. 39).)
2) How does Sephy feel about the decision Zeus has made? (She accepts the decision; she

doesn't mind so much now that she knows it is only for half the year (p. 41).)
3) How does Sephy feel towards Pluto by the end of the story? (She understands how lonely he is and she even begins to care for him. She decides that it is not his fault that he was made King of the Underworld (p. 42).)

Talk about the way in which Sephy's feelings towards Pluto have changed. What has happened to make her see him in a different light?

Discuss the way in which this story explains the seasons. How does the pattern of Sephy's life mirror the natural cycle of the seasons?

Reread pp. 43–44, focusing on the description of Sephy's ascent up the dark tunnels as she pushes up through the soil towards light and warmth; what do the images remind the children of? Compare Sephy's journey with the growth of a seedling trying to push its way through heavy soil to reach the warmth and light of the sun.

Notice how the author has again used a poetic style of writing in the final chapter. Look at the sentence that begins, "Round and up I go…" (p. 43) and discuss how this long, descriptive sentence is rather like a verse of poetry. Notice how sentences are broken down into shorter phrases by her effective use of punctuation.

Talk about the themes of compromise and acceptance. What do the group think about Zeus's decision? Is it a fair compromise? Do they think they would be as accepting about their fate as Sephy if they were in her shoes?

Next steps
Activity Sheet 5: "Demeter's Story" asks children to retell Sephy's story from the perspective of her mother, Demeter.

Demeter's Story

Retell Sephy's story in the words of her mother, Demeter.

The day started as usual. I worked in the vegetable garden while my daughter played in the fields. My daughter's name is Persephone, Sephy for short. She is such a pretty child, so full of life. She brings light and happiness wherever she goes…

_____

_____

_____

_____

_____

_____

_____

_____

_____

_____

_____

_____

_____

_____

White Wolves Teachers' Resource
for Guided Reading Year 3
Myths and Legends
© A & C Black 2007

Wings of Icarus by Jenny Oldfield

About the book

Daedalus and his son, Icarus, have been banished to the island of Crete by King Minos. Daedalus had angered the king by creating the Minotaur: a monster with the body of a man and the head of a bull.

Icarus longs to escape the island and Daedalus wonders how to give his son the gift of freedom. Icarus suggests that they build a boat. Daedalus is reluctant at first, but seeing his son's excitement, he draws up plans. Icarus helps his father construct the boat and, when the project is completed, they drag it to the water's edge and set off to sea. Before long, a storm breaks out, and by morning they are back where they had started – on the shore of their prison isle. Daedalus believes that the storm had been sent by King Minos to remind them that he is lord of the sea. He declares that, while King Minos may be lord of the sea and the earth, he is not lord of the sky. He tells Icarus that he will make wings and they will fly away like birds. Icarus eagerly accepts his father's new plans and helps by gathering feathers, which Daedalus attaches to a light, wooden frame using soft wax.

When the wings are complete, Daedalus straps the wings to his son's back, warning him not to dip too low towards the sea, and not to fly too close to the sun as the wax will melt and the feathers will fall from the frame. Icarus, impatient to fly free, soars into the sky and joins the birds in flight. Daedalus watches helplessly as Icarus flies close to the sun and is dazzled by its light. The sun melts the wax and the feathers begin to fall. Daedalus looks on as Icarus plummets into the sea and is drowned.

Chapter Four

The wind blew from the north as Daedalus and Icarus stepped into the boat.

"Unfurl the sail," Daedalus said, steadying himself at the rudder.

Icarus untied the strings and let the sail flap. The wind caught it; the boat jolted forward from the shore.

28

"It works!" Icarus gasped.

"Yes, it works," Daedalus echoed, tugging the rudder to steer the boat clear of some sharp rocks.

His son gazed ahead at the wide blue sea. He felt the wind in his hair, the sun on his face and a salty spray from the waves.

29

Wings of Icarus: Teaching Sequence 1

Summary of Chapter One

Icarus wonders what lies beyond the Aegean Sea; he imagines escaping from his island prison. That night he dreams about a monster with the body of a man and the head of an ugly bull: the Minotaur! Daedalus comforts his son and sits with him until the nightmare has faded. He was responsible for creating the bull-monster, which was the cause of their exile. Daedalus wonders how he and his son can escape.

Teaching Sequence

Introduction
Talk about the book cover and read the blurb.
- Point out that this story is a Greek myth. Find out about other myths the children are familiar with. What do they know about Greek gods, for example, Zeus?
- Look at the illustration on the front cover and discuss how it might relate to the book's title.

Independent reading
Ask the group to read Chapter One, focusing on reading for meaning.
- Help with the pronunciation of the names Icarus, Daedalus, Minotaur, King Minos and Pasiphae.
- Discuss less familiar words and phrases such as *Aegean Sea* (p. 5), *slain, henceforth, exile* (p. 12), *banished, in vain* (p. 13).

Returning to the text
Develop children's understanding of the story by asking some of these questions either during reading or at the end of the chapter. Encourage them to find the relevant part in the text to support their answers.
1) What is Icarus thinking about when he stares out at the Aegean Sea? (He wonders what lies beyond the water (p. 5); he cannot leave the island because he has been exiled there.)
2) What similes has the author used to describe the shell given to Icarus by his father? (It's smooth and shiny as polished marble (p. 6). When Icarus holds it to his ear he hears a sound, like distant waves breaking on the shore (p. 7).)
3) What is the Minotaur? (It is a monster with the body of a man and the ugly head of a bull (p. 9); a "bull-monster" (p. 11).)
4) Why does Daedalus feel troubled? (He feels to blame for Icarus being banished on the island with him, and he wishes he could find a way to give his son the freedom he longs for (p. 13).)

Talk about the punishment that King Minos inflicted on Daedalus and his son. Was it fair? Is it fair to punish Icarus for his father's actions? Should the king have forgiven Daedalus after he had killed the monster? Should any punishment last for ever?

Ask the children how they would feel about being banished to an island. What would they take with them? What would they miss the most?

Discuss the relationship between Daedalus and Icarus. Daedalus's desire to help his son is all-consuming. When Icarus has a nightmare, he rushes to his side. Icarus may appear independent, but his need for his father is displayed in this episode, too.

Ask a volunteer to role-play the part of Daedalus. The other members of the group can interview him about the time when he trapped and killed the Minotaur. What was the creature like? How did he trap it? What did he use to destroy it?

Next steps
The children can now complete Activity Sheet 1: "The Minotaur", which asks them to write a descriptive passage about the time when Daedalus trapped and killed the Minotaur.

The Minotaur

Write a short prequel to *Wings of Icarus*. Describe what happened when Daedalus trapped and killed the Minotaur.

- Describe how the Minotaur looked.
- Explain how Daedalus trapped the monster in a maze.
- Describe how Daedalus destroyed the monster.
- What happened next?
- What was Daedalus hoping would happen?

_____

_____

_____

_____

_____

_____

_____

_____

_____

_____

_____

_____

_____

White Wolves Teachers' Resource
for Guided Reading Year 3
Myths and Legends
© A & C Black 2007

Wings of Icarus: Teaching Sequence 2

Summary of Chapter Two

Daedalus finds his son swimming in the sea. When Icarus arrives back on dry land, Daedalus observes that he is an "almost-man", a boy afraid of bad dreams in one breath, and proud and reckless in the next. Daedalus is frustrated that, despite being the greatest inventor in all of Athens, he cannot find a way to escape the island. Icarus loves his father, and he loves the sunny island of Crete, but the two are not enough to keep him happy.

Teaching Sequence

Introduction
Recap on the events of Chapter One. Why are Icarus and his son prisoners on Crete?

Independent reading
Ask the group to read aloud Chapter Two, focusing on reading for meaning.
- Discuss less familiar words such as *horizon* (p. 14), *current* (p. 16), *reckless, almost-man, rival* (p. 17), *roosted* (p. 19).

Returning to the text
Develop children's understanding of the story by asking some of these questions either during reading or at the end of the chapter. Encourage them to find the relevant part in the text to support their answers.
1) What concerns does Daedalus have about his son? (He is gone for hours. When he finds him, Icarus is far out at sea, where the current could carry him away.)
2) What does the author mean by the expression "he bit his tongue" (p. 17)?
3) What do the author's descriptions of the landscape tell us about the island? (The author refers to a seashore, high rocks and clear pools (p. 14), olive trees on a lonely hill (p. 17), low trees (p. 18), and the dark maze with a tower at its centre (p. 19). Icarus finds the island oppressive and confining.)
4) In what ways are Daedalus and Icarus different and in what ways are they similar? (For example, Daedalus shows that he, too, is proud when he reflects that he has invented great wonders: "In all of Athens there was no inventor clever enough to rival me" (p. 17).)

Talk about the rich language used to describe simple actions. For example, "With his head bowed and his gaze fixed on stony ground, he walked slowly into the sunset" (p. 18). In describing the way Daedalus walks, the author shows the reader how he is feeling. Similarly, she reveals Icarus's feelings when she describes him "striding away angrily as the red sun sank into the sea" (p. 19).

Note the author's use of personification in her description of the "lonely hill". Discuss how this reflects the way Daedalus is feeling as he walks among the olive trees.

Ask children to find adverbs that the author has used in Chapter Two, for example, "proudly", "slowly", "angrily". Discuss what additional information these words give the reader.

Discuss the variety of emotions expressed by the two characters in Chapter Two, for example, concern, pride, frustration, love, anger. Explore the characters' emotions further through role-play. The group could hot-seat Icarus, asking him about the way he feels and why he is discontented.

Next steps
Activity Sheet 2: "Message in a Bottle" asks children to imagine they are Icarus and write about themselves, the island they live on, and their greatest wish.

Message in a Bottle

Imagine you are Icarus. You have found a piece of parchment, a quill and a bottle. If you write a message and seal it inside the bottle, the current will carry it out to sea and it may be found by someone living beyond the water.

- What message will you write?
- Write a little about yourself.
- Describe the island you are living on.
- What will you wish for above all else?

_____

_____

_____

_____

_____

_____

_____

_____

_____

_____

_____

_____

_____

White Wolves Teachers' Resource
for Guided Reading Year 3
Myths and Legends
© A & C Black 2007

Wings of Icarus: Teaching Sequence 3

Summary of Chapter Three

Icarus suggests that they build a boat. Daedalus is reluctant at first as he is too old and weak to row very far and Icarus is only a boy but, seeing his son's excitement, he draws up plans. Icarus helps his father construct the boat and, after many hot days, the project is completed. The finishing touch is a sail. Daedalus explains how his invention will enable the wind to carry the boat across the waves.

Teaching Sequence

Introduction
Ask the children to remind you about the events of the previous chapter. How would Daedalus describe his son? Why is Icarus dissatisfied?

Independent reading
Ask the group to read aloud Chapter Three, focusing on reading for meaning.
- Discuss less familiar words and phrases such as *condemned* (p. 20), *hasty* (p. 21), *embers, parchment, quill* (p. 22), *stoutest timbers, fashion, beams, dusk* (p. 23), *framework, vessel* (p. 24), *uneasy, distant horizon* (p. 25), *billow* (p. 26), *erect, sail* (p. 27).

Returning to the text
Develop children's understanding of the story by asking some of these questions either during reading or at the end of the chapter. Encourage them to find the relevant part in the text to support their answers.
1) Whose idea was it to build a boat? (Icarus's (p. 21).)
2) Why is Daedalus uneasy about Icarus's idea to escape the island by boat? (He wonders who will row the boat as he is old and weak (p. 22), and Icarus is just a boy (p. 25).)
3) What materials do they use to build their boat?

(Stout timbers, iron nails, a square of cloth.)
4) What was Daedalus's invention for carrying the boat across the sea and how did it work? (He invented a sail using a pole and a square of cloth (p. 26); when the wind blows it catches the sail and propels the boat across the water.)

Ask the children to point out words and phrases the author has used to describe Daedalus and Icarus in Chapter Two. For example, Icarus is "excited", "hasty" and "full of hope", whereas Daedalus is "uneasy". Icarus is quick to act, whereas Daedalus puzzles over things until he finds the answer.

Ask the group if they think age has anything to do with the differences between the two characters. Might Daedalus have been more like his son when he was younger? Perhaps age has taught him to be less hasty? Remind the group that Daedalus is responsible for them being trapped on the island; his creation of the Minotaur could be considered foolish.

The children could sketch and label a design for a boat. Ask them to make a list of the resources they would need and remind them to think about what materials might have been available to them on an ancient Greek island so that their designs are in keeping with the time and place.

The group could hot-seat each of the characters in turn. They could ask Icarus to describe how he feels about his father. They could ask Daedalus what he loves about Icarus and what he finds frustrating about him.

Next steps
The children can now complete Activity Sheet 3: "Father and Son", which asks children to think about how the characters Daedalus and Icarus would describe one another.

Father and Son

Write what you think Daedalus and Icarus would say about one another. Think carefully about the different words they might use to describe each other.

> I love my son, Icarus, dearly, but I am worried about him…

> I love my father very much, but I wish he hadn't angered King Minos and condemned us to living on this island for ever! My father is a very clever man…

White Wolves Teachers' Resource
for Guided Reading Year 3
Myths and Legends
© A & C Black 2007

Wings of Icarus: Teaching Sequence 4

Summary of Chapter Four

Daedalus and Icarus set off, but before long waves lash against the boat and tear the sail, leaving them at the mercy of the sea. By morning, they are back where they had started. Icarus puts away his shell and no longer listens to the song of the sea. Daedalus studies his parchments, hoping to find a way to restore his son's hope. Finally he tells Icarus that they will make wings and fly away like birds. Icarus eagerly accepts his father's new plans and helps by gathering feathers.

Teaching Sequence

Introduction

Recap briefly on the events of Chapter Three. Do the children think that Daedalus and Icarus will be successful in their attempt to escape?

Independent reading

Ask the group to read aloud Chapter Four, focusing on reading for meaning.

- Discuss less familiar words and phrases such as *unfurl, rudder, jolted* (p. 28), *mercy* (p. 30), *craggy, isle* (p. 31), *battlements* (p. 33), *soar, down-soft feathers* (p. 34).

Returning to the text

Develop children's understanding of the story by asking some of these questions either during reading or at the end of the chapter. Encourage them to find the relevant part in the text to support their answers.

1) How do you think Daedalus and Icarus were feeling when their boat left the shore? (Icarus might be euphoric and excited, while Daedalus is delighted to be granting his son's wish, but anxious about the dangers that lie ahead.)

2) What happened when the weather changed? (The wind grew stronger and waves lashed against the boat, tearing the sail apart.)

3) Who does Daedalus think is to blame for his failure to escape the island by boat? (He blames King Minos, who he believes sent the storm to show that he is lord of the sea (p. 32).)

4) How do Daedalus and Icarus behave following their failed attempt to escape by boat? (Icarus despairs; he puts away his shell and no longer listens to the sound of the sea (p. 32). Daedalus studies his parchments and sets about finding a new answer (p. 32).)

Look at the author's personification of the sea on p. 30: "The waves lashed against the boat … leaving them at the mercy of the angry sea". Focus on other examples of descriptive words and phrases, and ask the group to pick out their favourite examples.

Discuss the change of heart in Daedalus. Earlier in the story he had been reluctant to help his son escape the island by boat, as he had doubts about their ability to navigate the strong current. His anger at King Minos, however, has brought about a new resolve in him. It had been Icarus's idea to build a boat, but Daedalus comes up with the plan to construct wings and escape the island by air. Daedalus's love for his son is, as always, the driving force.

Next steps

The children can now complete Activity Sheet 4: "Daedalus & Son: Latest Inventions", which asks them to write advertisements for Daedalus's boats and wings.

Daedalus & Son: Latest Inventions

Daedalus is known all over Greece for his great inventions. Help him to write advertisements for his latest wonders.

Set sail in the latest sea model: DAEDALUS I

EXPERTLY CRAFTED!

_____

_____

_____

_____

_____

_____

Take flight with the ICARUS winged harness

HAND MADE!

_____

_____

_____

_____

_____

_____

White Wolves Teachers' Resource
for Guided Reading Year 3
Myths and Legends
© A & C Black 2007

Wings of Icarus: Teaching Sequence 5

Summary of Chapter Five

Daedalus finishes the work on his latest invention, as Icarus sleeps. In the morning, Daedalus takes his son to the top of the tower where they watch the birds flying, learning how they beat their wings to catch the currents of air. Then Daedalus straps the wings to his son's back, warning him not to dip too low towards the sea and not to fly too close to the sun. Without waiting for his father, Icarus soars into the sky and joins the birds in flight. Daedalus watches helplessly as Icarus flies too close to the sun. The sun melts the wax and the feathers begin to fall. Daedalus looks on as Icarus plummets into the sea and is drowned.

Teaching Sequence

Introduction

Ask the group to remind you of Daedalus's latest plan to escape the island. How do they think the story will end? Will Icarus and his father be successful in their attempt to escape this time?

Independent reading

Ask the group to read aloud Chapter Five, focusing on reading for meaning.

- Discuss less familiar words and phrases, such as *soared* (p. 38), *burning orb* (p. 42), *falter*, *plummeted down* (p. 43).

Returning to the text

Develop children's understanding of the story by asking some of these questions either during reading or at the end of the chapter. Encourage them to find the relevant part in the text to support their answers.

1) Why do Daedalus and Icarus spend time watching birds from the top of the tower? (They want to learn how birds fly by beating their wings to catch the currents of air (p. 37).)
2) Is Icarus nervous about flying? (No, he can hardly wait; he is impatient for his father to strap the wings to his back, asking him to "be quick" and "hurry".)
3) What dangers does Daedalus want his son to be aware of? (He warns Icarus not to dip close to the sea, because his wings will not carry him back up to the sky if they get wet, and not to fly too close to the sun as it will melt the wax and the feathers will fall off.)

Ask the group to look for words that the author has used in place of the often over-used word "said", for example "warned", "pleaded", "cautioned", "begged", "told", "cried", "sighed", "whispered". Discuss how, in addition to making the narrative more interesting, the author gives extra information to the reader through her word choices. Ask the children to notice pairs of words that are similar in meaning (synonyms), for example, pleaded / begged; warned / cautioned.

Think about the character of Icarus. Was he to blame for his own downfall or was it his father's responsibility to keep him safe from harm? Would someone of a less impetuous nature have heeded their father's words and avoided danger? Icarus did not answer his father when he warned him to "take care"; did he choose to ignore the warning, or was he too caught up in the excitement of flying to hear it?

Talk about the tragic ending. Did the children expect it? Were there any clues that events would lead to this? Discuss also the way the author helps create the tragedy, for example, by concentrating on the relationship between father and son throughout the story.

Next steps

Activity Sheet 5 gives children an opportunity to think about the author's word choices in relation to the frequently over-used word "said".

Instead of "said"

The author of *Wings of Icarus* has chosen words very carefully to avoid repetition and to make the story as interesting as possible.

Read this extract from the story and write a verb in each space. Avoid using the word "said". Then compare the words you have chosen with those used by the author in the book.

Daedalus came and strapped the wings to his son's back. "Take care not to dip too low towards the sea," he _____. "If your wings get wet, they will not carry you back up to the sky."

Icarus nodded. "Be quick, Father," he _____, as Daedalus buckled the straps.

"But do not fly too high," his father _____. For if you fly too close to the sun, it will melt the wax and the feathers will fall from the frame."

"Please hurry!" Icarus _____. As he spread his arms wide and the wind caught his wings, he heard the call of lands beyond the sea.

Meanwhile, Daedalus struggled to attach his own wings. "Wait until I am ready," he _____ his son. "We will fly together."

But Icarus already felt the power of the wind. He beat his wings and rose from the tower. His father looked up in fear. "Take care Icarus!"

Icarus did not answer. He beat his wings again and soared into the air, joining the birds of the sky. Daedalus watched, helpless, as Icarus rose higher towards the sun. "come back!" he _____.

What other words might a writer use instead of "said"? Use a thesaurus to help you find some interesting alternatives.

_____

_____

_____

Record Card

Group:	Book:

Focus for Session:

Names	Comments

The White Wolves Interview:
Rose Impey

Rose Impey has written over 100 books for children of all ages: picture books like *A Letter to Father Christmas*, series books including *Colour Crackers* and *Titchy Witch* and novels for older readers such as *My Scary Fairy Godmother*. She also created **The Sleepover Club** series, which was adapted for TV.

Rose lives in Leicester in a cottage with a walled garden, where she enjoys gardening and relaxing.

Would you describe yourself as a curious person?

I would definitely describe myself as a curious person, I think all writers are. I'd even go so far as to say I was downright nosy. I love to know exactly what other people are doing, saying, thinking. I'll listen in to other people's conversations given half a chance. It's how you learn what makes other people tick.

Do you think curiosity is a weakness or a strength?

So I would have to say that curiosity is a strength. I often tell children it's one of two qualities I think a writer needs. The other one is stubbornness. It's far too easy to give up otherwise. And it's interesting, isn't it, that those are two things children are often told they shouldn't be!

If you were a Greek god or goddess, which one would you be and why?

If I were a Greek goddess I'd probably choose to be Demeter because she looked after the countryside, making sure the crops were ready. I'm a really passionate gardener so that would suit me very well.

How does retelling a classic story in a new way compare with writing a story from scratch?

Retelling makes a pleasant change from writing original stories because it allows you to concentrate entirely on the telling and the style of the story instead of having to worry about the plot.

What sort of stories do you enjoy reading?

I enjoy reading stories about real people living real lives. I like stories that make me laugh and those that make me cry, but most importantly they must contain characters that I care about and want to spend all that time with.

The White Wolves Interview:
Julia Green

Julia Green writes mainly for young adults. *Blue Moon*, *Baby Blue* and *Hunter's Heart* are published by Puffin.

She lives in Bath with her two teenage children, and lectures in creative writing at Bath Spa University. She is programme leader for the MA in Writing for Young People. She also runs writing workshops for young people and adults.

What is your favourite season and why?

My favourite season is spring: I love it when the first snowdrops appear in my garden, and then the daffodils, and later on the first fresh green leaves on the trees. It's a hopeful time, life bursting out everywhere in nature.

I like it when the days start getting longer – the light changes, the birds sing more. I always notice these things. My children were born in the spring, too – March, and May, so these are special months to me.

If you were a Greek god or goddess, who would you be and why?

I think I'd like to be Demeter, because I love growing things. (Raspberries and redcurrants are my favourite at the moment: I grow them on my allotment.) I do quite like the idea of having wings, though, so it might be fun to be Hermes.

How does retelling a classic story in a new way compare with writing a story from scratch?

Retelling a classic story is great, because the characters and storyline are already there, which frees me up to think about how to tell that story. My job is to think of a new way of telling it to make it fresh. With *Sephy's Story*, I thought I'd tell it in the first person, from Persephone's viewpoint. That made me think hard about how to tell the bits of the story which happen when Sephy isn't there to see what's happening. It's a challenge. I like that. I feel I have to do justice to the original story, and I want to use words in interesting ways. It's more restricting than making up my own story from scratch, though. I like doing both. I like making up my own characters, and seeing what's going to happen to them.

What sort of stories do you enjoy reading?

I love reading all sorts of stories. When I was a child, I read all the time! I loved a story called *Tom's Midnight Garden*, and *The Borrowers*, and *The Children of Green Knowe*. They were mostly stories about real, believable people, but with some magical element, too. I liked animal stories as well: *Tarka the Otter*, and *Black Beauty*. I absolutely loved the books by Laura Ingalls Wilder about her life growing up in the woods and prairies in America. I didn't read the Greek myths until much later, when I was grown up. I still read all the time.

The White Wolves Interview:
Jenny Oldfield

Jenny Oldfield was born in Yorkshire, where she still lives with her two daughters, Kate and Eve. She read English at university and then pursued a number of jobs before she started writing at the age of 24. She has now published over 50 books for adults and children, many in popular series including *My Magical Pony* and *Definitely Daisy*. Jenny has always loved the outdoors and when she isn't writing, she loves horse riding, playing tennis, walking and travelling to far-off places.

Describe the place where you like to write.
I can only write in one particular room – a first-floor study at the back of my house, overlooking the river and a wooded hillside. If I'm working, the door is closed and nobody disturbs me!

If you were exiled to live on a Greek island for ever, what would you take with you and what would you miss most?
Exile on a Greek island is my idea of paradise!

Golden sun and sand, endless blue sea. The object I would take with me (this is like Desert Island Discs!) would be a family photograph. The thing I would miss the most – my family!

How does retelling a classic story in a new way compare with writing a story from scratch?
Retelling a classic story is like having a scaffold of steel bars. My own words are the bricks that make the building inhabitable. It's a very enjoyable, creative process.

What sort of stories do you enjoy reading?
I enjoy reading stories about underdogs – people who are overlooked or mistreated, who survive through their own courage and resourcefulness. It can be any setting, any period, any style of story, but it must have a hero or heroine who works his / her way out of darkness into the light.

White Wolves Resources for Guided Reading

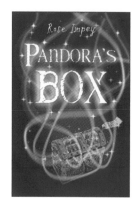

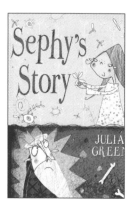

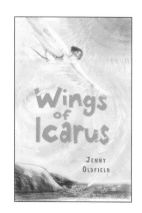

White Wolves Resources for Guided Reading

Year 4

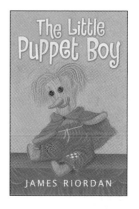

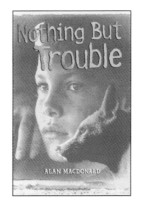

White Wolves Resources for Guided Reading

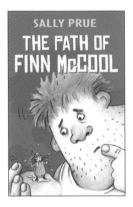

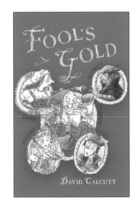

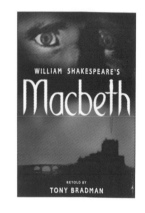

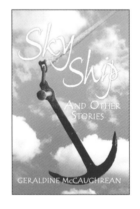

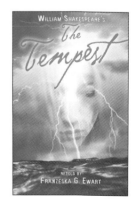